IN THE MARGINS

IN THE MARGINS

ON THE PLEASURES OF
READING AND WRITING

ELENA FERRANTE

Translated from the Italian by
Ann Goldstein

THORNDIKE PRESS
A part of Gale, a Cengage Company

GALE
A Cengage Company

**LIBRARY OF CONGRESS CIP DATA ON FILE.
CATALOGUING IN PUBLICATION FOR THIS BOOK
IS AVAILABLE FROM THE LIBRARY OF CONGRESS.**

ISBN-13: 978-1-4328-9546-4 (hardcover alk. paper)

Published in 2022 by arrangement with Europa Editions Inc.

Printed in Mexico
Print Number: 01   Print Year: 2022

CONTENTS

CONTENTS

EDITOR'S NOTE

This book originated in an email from Professor Costantino Marmo, director of the Centro Internazionale di Studi Umanistici Umberto Eco. It read, in part:

> I like to think that the autumn of 2020 would be the ideal time for Elena Ferrante to give three lectures at the University of Bologna, on three successive days, open to the entire city. These lectures would discuss her work as a

writer, her poetics, her narrative technique, or anything else she wants, and would ideally be of interest to a broad, non-specialist audience.

The Eco Lectures belong to a tradition of lectures given by figures from the national and international world of culture which Umberto Eco, then director of the Scuola Superiore di Studi Umanistici, decided to offer the university and the city of Bologna in the early years of this century. The first series was given by Elie Wiesel (in January of 2000), the most recent by Orhan Pamuk (in the spring of 2014).

Then came the pandemic and the

lockdowns, and public events were impossible. In the meantime, however, Ferrante, having accepted the invitation, had written the three lectures. And so in November of 2021 the actress Manuela Mandracchia, in the guise of Elena Ferrante, presented the lectures at the Teatro Arena del Sole in Bologna, together with ERT, Emilia Romagna Teatro.

The author's exploration of reading and writing continues here with *Dante's Rib,* an essay composed at the invitation of the ADI, the Association of Italianists, under the auspices of Professor Alberto Casadei and the president of the ADI, Gino Ruozzi. The essay concluded the conference Dante and Other

Classics (April 29, 2021), where it was read by the scholar and critic Tiziana de Rogatis.

Sandra Ozzola

■ ■ ■ ■

PAIN AND PEN

■ ■ ■ ■

Ladies and gentlemen, this evening I'm going to talk to you about the desire to write and about the two kinds of writing it seems to me I know best, the first compliant, the second impetuous. But I will begin, if I may, by devoting a few lines to a child I'm very fond of and her first attempts at the alphabet.

Recently Cecilia — as I will call her here — wanted to show me how well she was able to write her name. I gave her a pen and a sheet of paper from the printer, and she commanded: Watch. Then, with intense concentration, she wrote "Cecilia" — letter by letter, in capitals — her eyes narrowed as if she were facing some danger. I was pleased, but also a little anxious. Once or twice I thought: Now I'll help her, guide her hand — I didn't want her to make a mistake. But she did it all by herself. She didn't worry in the least about starting off at the top of the page. She aimed sometimes up, sometimes down, assigning the letters — each consonant, each vowel — random dimensions, one big, one small, one medium-sized, leaving a lot of space between the individual marks. Finally she turned to me

14

and, almost shouting, said, See?, with an imperative need to be praised.

Naturally I feted her — effusively — but I felt a little uneasy. Why that fear that she would make a mistake? Why that impulse of mine to guide her hand? I've thought about it lately. Surely, many decades earlier, I, too, had written in the same irregular manner, on some random piece of paper, with the same concentration, the same apprehension, the same need for praise. But, in all honesty, I have to say I have no memory of doing so. My first memories of writing have to do with elementary-school notebooks. They had — I don't know if they still do — horizontal black lines, unevenly spaced, so that they defined areas of different sizes. Like this:

Dettato

Prova a leggere in fretta queste
parole:

Questo e quello, quando e
quanto, quinci e quindi, qualche
e quale, quinto e quivi, quattro
e quarto, quercia e quiete,
quasi e quadro, quanti e

The size of these areas changed from first grade to fifth. If you disciplined your hand and learned to line up small, round letters and letters that ascended or descended, you passed, and the horizontal segments that divided the page got smaller from year to year until they became, in fifth grade, a single line. Like this:

Geografia

I

La Terra.

La Terra é il pianeta, che noi abitiamo, ha la forma di una sfera e dista dal sole ch'é la piú grande stella 150 milioni di chilometri.

Noi la rappresentiamo col globo dove sono segnati l'asse, l'equatore, i paralleli ed i meridiani.

L'asse é la linea immaginaria intorno a cui gira la terra. L'estremitá dell'asse che sta in alto si chiama polo nord. L'estremitá dell'asse, che sta in basso si chiama polo sud.

L'equatore é quel circolo massimo, che passando per il centro della terra la divide in due parti, cioé emisfero nord ed emisfero sud. I meridiani sono circoli massimi che passando per i poli divide la terra in due parti, cioé emisfero orientale ed emisfero occidentale.

I paralleli sono circoli minori e paralleli all'equatore che si impiccioliscono a mano, a mano che si avvicinano ai poli.

You were big by now — you had begun your school journey at six and now you were ten — and you were big because your writing flowed in an orderly way across the page.

Flowed where? Well, defining the white page were not only the horizontal black lines but two vertical red lines, one on the left, one on the right. The writing was supposed to move between those lines, and those lines — of this I have a very clear memory — tormented me. They were intended to indicate, by their color as well, that if your writing didn't stay between those taut lines you would be punished. But I was easily distracted when I wrote, and while I almost always respected the margin on the left, I often ended up outside the one on the right, whether to finish the word or because I had reached a point where it was difficult to divide the word into syllables and start a new line without going outside the margin. I was punished so often that the sense of the boundary became part of me, and when I write by hand I feel the threat of the vertical red line even though I haven't used paper like that for years.

What to say? Today I suspect that my writing — let's say — like Cecilia's, ended up in or under the writing in those notebooks. I don't remember it, and yet it must be there, educated at last to stay on the lines and between the margins.

Probably that first effort is the matrix from which I still get a self-congratulatory sense of victory whenever something obscure suddenly emerges from invisibility to become visible, thanks to a sequence of marks on the page or the computer screen. It's a provisional alphabetical combination, surely imprecise, but I have it before my eyes, very close to the brain's first impulses and yet here, outside, already detached. There is such a childish magic to this that if I had to symbolize its energy in graphic form I would use the disorderly way Cecilia wrote her name, insisting that I watch her and in those letters see her and enthusiastically recognize her.

In my longing to write, starting in early adolescence, both the threat of those red lines — my handwriting now is very neat, and when I'm using the computer I go, after a paragraph or so, to the alignment icon and click on the option that evens the margins — and the desire and fear of violating them are probably at work. More generally, I believe that the sense I have of writing — and all the struggles it involves — has to do with the satisfaction of staying beautifully within the margins and, at the same time, with the impression of loss, of waste, because of that success.

I started with a child trying to write her name, but now, to continue, I'd like to invite you to look for a moment between the lines of Zeno Cosini, the protagonist of Italo Svevo's greatest book, *Zeno's Conscience.* We're catching Zeno right in the effort of writing, and his effort, in my eyes, isn't that far from Cecilia's.

Now, having dined, comfortably lying in my overstuffed lounge chair, I am holding a pencil and a piece of paper. My brow is unfurrowed because I have dismissed all concern from my mind. My thinking seems something separate from me. I can see it. It rises and falls . . . but that is its only activity. To remind it that it is my thinking and that its duty is to

24

make itself evident, I grasp the pencil. Now my brow does wrinkle, because each word is made up of so many letters and the imperious present looms up and blots out the past.

(Translated by William Weaver)

Not infrequently the writer starts the story at the very moment when he is preparing to carry out his task; in fact I would say that it's always been like that. The way we see ourselves dragging outside, by means of the written word, an imaginary "inside," which is by its nature fleeting, deserves more attention in discussions of literature. I have felt its fascination, I obsessively collect instances of it. And this passage of Svevo has always impressed me, since I was a girl. I wrote all the time, even if it was laborious and almost always disappointing. When I read that passage, I was convinced that Zeno Cosini had problems like mine, but knew a lot more about them.

Svevo, as you've heard, makes the point that everything begins with pencil and paper. Then a surprising split takes place: the I of the writer separates from its own thought and, in the separation, sees that thought. It's not a fixed, well-defined image. The thought-vision appears as something in motion — it rises and falls — and its task is to make itself evident before disappearing. The verb is precisely that, "make evident," and, significantly, it refers to an action carried out by the hand. The something that the I sees — something moving, therefore alive — has to be "grasped by the hand" holding the pencil and transformed on the piece of paper into a written word. It seems like an easy operation, but Zeno's brow, smooth before, wrinkles; it's no small struggle. Why? Here Svevo makes an observation that is important to me. The struggle is due to the fact that the present — the entire present, even that of the "I" who writes, letter by letter — can't maintain with clarity the thought-vision, which always comes before, is always the past, and therefore tends to be blotted out.

I read those few lines, I took out the irony, I adapted them, I applied them to myself. And I imagined that I was in a race against time, a race in which the writer always lagged behind. While, in fact, the letters were rapidly lining up next to one another, asserting themselves, the vision fled, and writing was destined to a frustrating approximation. It was too slow to capture the brain wave. The "so many letters" were slow, they strove to capture the past while they themselves became the past, and much was lost. When I reread myself, I had the impression that a voice flitting around my head was carrying more than what had actually become letters.

■ ■ ■ ■

I don't recall ever thinking, when I was young, that I was inhabited by an alien voice. No, that bad feeling I never experienced. But things became complicated when I wrote. I read a lot, but what I liked was almost always written by men, not women. It seemed to me that the voice of men came from the pages, and that voice preoccupied me, I tried in every way to imitate it. Even when I was around thirteen — just to hold on to a clear memory — and had the impression that my writing was good, I felt that someone was telling me what should be written and how. At times he was male but invisible. I didn't even know if he was my age or grown up, perhaps old. More generally, I have to confess, I imagined becoming male yet at the same time remaining female. This impression, luckily, disappeared almost completely with the end of adolescence. I say "almost" because, even if the male voice had departed, there was a residual stumbling block: the impression that my woman's brain held me back, limited me, like a congenital slowness. Not only was writing difficult in itself but I was a girl and so would never be able to write books like those of the great writers. The quality of the writing in those books, their power, fired me with ambitions, dictated intentions that seemed far beyond my possibilities.

Then, maybe at the end of high school, I don't remember exactly when, completely by chance I came across the *Rime* of Gaspara Stampa, and one sonnet in particular made a deep impression. I understand now that she was using one of the great clichés of the poetic tradition: the insufficiency of language in the face of love, whether love of another human being or love of God. But at the time I didn't know that, and I was captivated by the way she expressed lovesickness and the written word in a continuous cycle, which led her, inevitably, to discover the disparity between the poem and the subject of the poem, or, in one of her formulas, between the living object that kindles the fire of love and "the mortal tongue encased in human flesh." The lines, which I read as if they were addressed directly to me, are these:

If, a lowly, abject woman, I
can carry within so sublime a
   flame,
why shouldn't I draw out at least
a little of its style and vein to
   show the world?
If love has lit a new and
   unheard-of spark
to raise me up to a place I'd
   never gained,
why, with equally uncommon
   skill,

can't it make my pen and pain
   the same?
And if the force of sheer nature's
   not
enough, why then some miracle
   that often
conquers, breaks, and ruptures
   every limit.
How this could be, I can't exactly
   say;
I know only that my great
   destiny's
impressed upon my heart a
   sweet new style.
       (Translated by Jane Tylus)

Later, I studied Gaspara Stampa
more systematically. But at the
time, as you see, that declaration in
the first line struck me immedi-

ately, "lowly, abject woman." If I, Gaspara said to me, I who feel that I am a woman to throw out, a woman without any value, am still capable of containing in myself a flame of love so sublime, why shouldn't I have at least a little inspiration and some beautiful words to give shape to that fire and show it to the world? If Love, lighting a new, unheard-of spark, has raised me up high, to a place that had been inaccessible to me, why can't it violate the usual rules of the game, and allow my pen to find words that will reproduce, as truly as possible, the pain of my love? And if Love can't count on nature, couldn't it perform a miracle, one of those which can break through any existing limit? I can't say precisely how it happened; but I can prove that a new style has been impressed on my heart.

At the time I also considered myself a lowly, abject woman. I was afraid, as I said, that it was precisely my female nature that kept me from bringing the pen as close as possible to the pain I wanted to express. For a woman who has something to say, does it really take a miracle — I said to myself — to dissolve the margins within which nature has enclosed her and show herself in her own words to the world?

Time passed, I read many other writers, and I realized that Gaspara Stampa was doing something completely new: she didn't confine herself to utilizing the great cliché of male poetic culture — the arduous reduction of the immeasurable pain of love to the measure of the pen — but grafted onto it something unexpected: the female body that fearlessly seeks, from the "mortal tongue," from within her own "human flesh," a garment of words sewn with a pain of her own and a pen of her own. Given that between pain and pen, for the male as well as the female, there remains a sort of innate imbalance, here was Stampa saying to me that the female pen, precisely because it is unexpected within the male tradition, had to make an enormous, courageous effort — five centuries ago, as today — to employ "uncommon skill" and acquire "style and vein."

At this point — I was around twenty, I think — a sort of vicious circle established itself clearly in my mind: if I wanted to believe that I was a good writer, I had to write like a man, staying strictly within the male tradition; although I was a woman, I couldn't write like a woman except by violating what I was diligently trying to learn from the male tradition.

From then on, for decades, I wrote and wrote, locked in that circle. I would start from something that seemed urgent, absolutely mine, and go on for days, weeks, sometimes months. Although the effects of the initial impulse faded, I kept going, the writing continued to advance, every line constructed and reconstructed. But the compass that had directed me had lost its needle; I seemed to be lingering on every word because I didn't know where to go. I will tell you something that may seem contradictory. When I finished a story, I was pleased, having the impression that it had come out perfectly; and yet I felt that it wasn't I who had written it — that is, not the excited I, ready for anything, who was called to write, and who during the entire draft had seemed to be hidden in the words — but another I, who, tightly disciplined, had found convenient pathways solely in order to say: look, see what fine sentences I've written, what beautiful images, the story is finished, praise me.

It was here that I began to think explicitly of having two kinds of writing: one that had been mine since my school years, and which had always assured me praise from the teachers (Brava, you'll be a writer someday); and another that peeped out by surprise and then vanished, leaving me unhappy. Over the years that unhappiness took different forms, but in essence it's still there.

I feel cramped, uncomfortable, in the well-balanced, calm, and compliant writing that made me think I knew how to write. To stick with

Gaspara Stampa's image of the spark that triggers the shot, modernizing the old Cupid's arrow, with that writing I kindle the spark that lights the gunpowder and open fire. But I realize that my bullets don't travel far. So I look for a more impetuous style, but — can't be helped — it seldom takes off. It appears, as far as I can tell, in the first lines, but I can't sustain it, and it disappears. Or it erupts after pages and pages and advances insolently, without tiring, without pausing, careless even of punctuation, strong only in its own vehemence. Then suddenly it leaves me. For much of my life I've written careful pages in the hope that they would be preliminary pages, and that the irrepressible burst would arrive, when the I writing from its fragment of the brain abruptly seizes all the possible I's, the entire head, the entire body, and, so empowered, begins to run, drawing into its net the world it needs. Those are wonderful moments. Something asks to become evident, said Svevo, to be grasped by the hand that writes. Something of me, a lowly, abject woman, said Gaspara Stampa, wants to leave the usual game and find vein and style. But in my experience that something easily eludes the grasp and is lost. Of course, you can recall it, you can even encapsulate it in a beautiful sentence, but the two moments — the moment it appeared and, right after that, the moment you started writing — either find the magical coordination that leads to the joy of writing or you have to be content to fiddle around with words, waiting for another dazzling occasion that will catch you more prepared, less distracted. It's one thing to plan a story and execute it well, another is that completely aleatoric writing, no less active than the world it tries to order. Now it erupts, now it disappears, now it's one alone, now it's a crowd, now it's small, whispered, now it gets huge and shouts. In other words it watches over, doubts, rolls, glitters, and meditates; it's like Mallarmé's proverbial throw of the dice.

I've often used some passages from Virginia Woolf's *A Writer's Diary* to get at the origin of this writing that eludes me. I would propose here, since time constrains us, only two excerpts, both very short but important to me. The first is a shred of apparently frivolous conversation with Lytton Strachey, who asks:

"And your novel?"
"Oh, I put in my hand and rummage in the bran pie."
"That's what's so wonderful. And it's all different."
"Yes, I'm 20 people."

That's it: the hand, the bran pie, twenty people. But, you see, in the space of a few self-mocking remarks there are two hints: first, the act of writing is a pure tempting of fate; second, what writing captures doesn't pass through the sieve of a singular I, solidly planted in every-day life, but is twenty people, that is, a number thrown out there to say: when I write, not even I know who I am. Certainly, Woolf states — and here is the second passage — I'm not Virginia:

It is a mistake to think that litera-ture can be produced from the raw. One must get out of life — yes, that's why I disliked so much the irruption of Sydney — one must become externalised; very, very concentrated, all at one point, not having to draw upon the scattered parts of one's character, living in the brain. Sydney comes and I'm Virginia; when I write I'm merely a sensibility. Sometimes I like being Virginia, but only when I'm scattered and various and gregarious. Now . . . I'd like to be only a sensibility.

Woolf's idea seems clear: writing is camping out in her own brain, without getting lost in the very numerous, varied, inferior modalities with which every day, as Virginia, she lives a raw life. It seemed to me, when I was young, that she was saying: oh yes, I like being Virginia, but the "I" who writes seriously isn't Virginia; the "I" who writes seriously is twenty people, a hypersensitive plurality all concentrated in the hand provided with the pen. The task of that hand is to rummage in the bran pie and pull out letters, words, phrases. True writing is the gesture that digs into the warehouse of literature in search of the necessary words. Not Virginia, therefore, which is the name of the raw life and the compliant writing. The writer has no name. She is pure sensibility that feeds on the alphabet and produces an alphabet within an uncontainable flow.

I am still fond of this image: an entity completely autonomous in relation to the biographically defined person (Virginia), which produces the written word in a separate space with extreme concentration. Except that it has become increasingly difficult for me to give it substance. Our impression is that writers talk about writing too often in an unsatisfying way. Think of when we say: the story tells itself, the character constructs him or her self, the language speaks to us, as if it were not us writing but someone else, who lives in us, tracing a course from the ancient world to our times: the god who dictates; the descent of the Holy Spirit; ecstasy; the encoded word in the unconscious; the network of relationships that we get caught in and each time modifies us, and so on. I've occasionally tried to clarify these ideas, but I haven't done so, returning instead to myself, to my two kinds of writing. They're not separate. The first, the usual, contains the second. If I deprived myself of it, I wouldn't write at all. It's writing that keeps me diligently within the margins, starting from those red lines in the elementary-school notebooks. Thanks to that writing I'm a prudent, perhaps timid (I've never had much courage — it's my cross) producer of pages that keep me within the rules I've learned. It's a permanent exercise, but if daily life becomes overinsistent, I can leave it without feeling too upset. Sometimes I say to myself that if Woolf's Virginia wrote, she would write with that same compliance.

The problem is the other writing, which Woolf prescribes for herself, defining it as a concentrated sensibility. Its center is, as for the first, in the brain — nothing but neurons. When I write I feel it, yet I don't know how to control it. The head doesn't know (maybe it doesn't want to know) how to free it conclusively, or even control its appearances. So my scribbling (this, too, is an expression I got long ago from Woolf) is mostly playing the usual game, waiting for the moment of true writing.

My work, in fact, is founded on patience. I start from writing that is planted firmly in tradition, and wait for something to erupt and throw the papers into disarray, for the lowly, abject woman I am to find a means of having her say. I adopt old techniques with pleasure; I've spent my life learning how and when to use them. I've always loved writing novels of love and betrayal, dangerous investigations, horrific discoveries, corrupted youth, miserable lives that have a stroke of luck. My adolescence as a reader became, without a break, a long and unhappy apprenticeship as an author. Literary genres are safe areas, solid platforms. There I can place a pale sketch of a story and practice with calm, wary pleasure. But really I am waiting for my brain to get distracted, to slip up, for other I's — many — outside the margins to join together, take my hand, begin to pull me with the writing where I'm afraid to go, where it hurts me to go, where, if I go too far, I won't necessarily know how to get back. It's the moment when the rules — learned, applied — give way and the hand pulls out of the bran pie not what is useful but, precisely, whatever comes, faster and faster, throwing me off balance.

Does that reliably produce good books? No, I don't think so. As far as I'm concerned, in the end not even this writing, despite the sense of frenetic power it conveys, fills the gap between pain and pen: it, too, leaves on the page less than what in the moment it seems to have

captured. Maybe, as with everything, you have to know how to
capture, restrain, contain it; that is,
know its merits and defects, learn
to use it. I haven't managed that
and I don't think I will. I've long
felt it only as an instrument of
destruction, a hammer that could
knock down the enclosure penning
me in. But destruction today seems
to me a rather ingenuous, avant-
garde-like project. Like all timid
and dutiful people, I had the un-
confessed and unconfessable ambi-
tion of going outside the given
forms, letting the writing spill outside them. Gradually that phase
passed: even Samuel Beckett, the
extraordinary Samuel Beckett, said
that the only thing we can't do

without, in literature and any other place, is form. So I got in the habit of using traditionally rigid structures and working on them carefully, while I waited patiently to start writing with all the truth I'm capable of, destabilizing, deforming, to make space for myself with my whole body. For me true writing is that: not an elegant, studied gesture but a convulsive act.

I cited Beckett for a reason. It's rare that someone who devotes his existence to writing hasn't left at least a few lines on the "I" stuck forcibly in a corner of the brain making written words. And I'm sure that in those lines there is not simply a sort of homage to the passion for writing but a door or gateway open onto the meaning of the writer's own work, its flaws and virtues. Now, in my view, Beckett, in *The Unnamable,* has done this best. The passage I propose is long, forgive me, but it could be even longer, maybe the whole book. Let's read:

I'm in words, made of words, others' words, what others, the place too, the air, the walls, the floor, the ceiling, all words, the whole world is here with me, I'm the air, the walls, the walled-in one, everything yields, opens, ebbs, flows, like flakes, I'm all these flakes, meeting, mingling, falling asunder, wherever I go I find me, leave me, go towards me, come from me, nothing ever but me, a particle of me, retrieved, lost, gone astray, I'm all these words, all these strangers, this dust of words, with no ground for their settling, no sky for their dispersing, coming together to say, fleeing one another to say, that I am they, all of them, those that merge, those that part, those that never meet, and nothing else, yes, something else, that I'm something quite different, a quite different thing, a wordless thing in an empty place, a hard shut dry cold black place, where nothing stirs, nothing speaks, and that I listen, and that I seek, like a caged beast born of caged beasts born of caged beasts born of caged beasts born in a cage and dead in a cage, born and then dead, born in a cage and then dead in a cage, in a word like a beast, in one of their words, like such a beast, and that I seek, like such a beast, with my little strength, such a beast, with nothing of its species left but fear and fury, no, the fury is past, nothing but fear . . .

In this orderly-disorderly din created by an I made exclusively of words — in this din that step by step leads back to the image of a long chain of caged beasts, motivated only by fear — I somewhat recognized myself. Before coming across it I had another image in mind, which originated with my mother: a whirlpool of fragment-words that made me feel sick, that scared me, and that, in my imagination, were the debris from a land submerged by the fury of the waters. A *frantumaglia,* my mother said, frightening herself, when she talked to me about her head, and frightening me so much that for a long time I preferred the image of the cage. At least it had secure boundaries, and it calmed me to feel that I was within a perimeter. I'm someone who generally closes the door behind me, and for a long time I preferred to resemble someone else rather than feel that I was without features. In a cage, the whirlpool of *frantumaglie* — which in recent years has reasserted itself — seemed to me more controllable.

The notebooks of elementary school were certainly a cage, with their horizontal black lines and vertical red ones. There, in fact, I began to put down little stories in writing, and since then I've tended to transform things into neat narratives, orderly, harmonious, successful. But the discordant clamor in my head remains; I know that the pages that finally persuade me to publish books come from there. Maybe what saves me — though it doesn't take much for salvation to be revealed as perdition — is that beneath the need for order is an enduring energy that will stumble, disarrange, delude, mistake, fail, soil. That energy pulls me every which way. Over time, writing has come to mean giving shape to a permanent balancing and unbalancing of myself, arranging fragments in a frame and waiting to mix them up. Thus the novel of love begins to satisfy me when it becomes the novel of being out of love. The mystery begins to absorb me when I know that no one will find out who the murderer is. The bildungsroman seems to me on the right track when it's clear that no one will be built. Beautiful writing becomes beautiful when it loses its harmony and has the desperate power of the ugly. And characters?

I feel they are false when they exhibit clear coherence and I become passionate about them when they say one thing and do the opposite. "Fair is foul and foul is fair," say those extraordinary narrators who are the witches in *Macbeth* as they prepare to hover through the fog and filthy air. But we'll talk about this and other things next time.

■ ■ ■ ■

AQUAMARINE

■ ■ ■ ■

Ladies and gentlemen, today I'd like to begin with a rule I made for myself at the age of sixteen or seventeen. The writer — I wrote in a notebook that I still have — has a duty to put into words the shoves he gives and those he receives from others. I reinforced this statement with a quotation: Tell the thing as it is, from *Jacques the Fatalist and His Master,* by Denis Diderot. I knew nothing at the time of Diderot's book; a teacher I liked had quoted the phrase to me once, as a piece of advice.

As a girl I had a passion for real things: I wanted to circumscribe, inscribe, describe, prescribe, even proscribe, if necessary. I couldn't contain myself, I was going to spill out into the world, into the other, into others, and write about them. I thought: everything that randomly kindles the start of a story is there outside and hits us, we collide, it confuses us, gets confused. Inside — inside us — is only the fragile machinery of our body. What we call "inner life" is a permanent flashing in the brain that wants to take shape as voice, as writing. So I looked around, waiting, for me at the time writing had, essentially, eyes: the trembling of a yellow leaf, the shiny parts of the coffee maker, my mother's ring with the aquamarine that gave off a sky-blue light, my sisters fighting in the courtyard, the enormous ears of the bald man in the blue smock. I wanted to be a mirror. I assembled fragments according to a before and an after, I set one inside the other, a story came out. It happened naturally, and I did it constantly.

Time passed and things got complicated. I began to be at war with myself: why this, why not this other, it's good, it's not good. Within a few years it seemed to me that I no longer knew how to write. Nothing I did could equal the books I liked, maybe because I was ignorant, maybe because I was inexperienced, maybe because I was a woman and therefore sentimental, maybe because I was stupid, maybe because I had no talent. Everything came to me as if fixed: the room, the window, society, good people, bad people, their clothes, their expressions, thoughts, objects that remained impassive even when they were handled. And then there were voices, the dialect of my city that in writing made me uneasy. As soon as I wrote it down, it sounded both remote from true dialect and jarring within the polished writing I was striving for.

I'd like to take a small example that I found in my notes of long ago: the aquamarine on my mother's finger. It was a real, very real, object, and yet there was nothing more variable in my mind. It shifted between dialect and Italian, in space and time, along with her figure, which was sometimes clear, sometimes murky, and always accompanied by my loving or hostile feelings. The aquamarine was changeable, part of a changing reality, a changing me. Even if I could isolate it in a description — how much I practiced descriptions! — and gave it a "sky-blue light," in that formulation alone the stone lost its substance, became an emotion of mine, a thought, a feeling of pleasure or distress, and turned opaque, as if it had fallen in water or I myself had breathed on it. That

opacity wasn't without conse-
quences; it tended almost imper-
ceptibly to raise my tone, as if in
that way I could restore luster to
the stone. Better, I said to myself,
to write a "pale celestial light." Or
forget light, just the color, "pale
celestial aquamarine." But I didn't
like the sound of it. I rummaged in
the dictionary and pulled out cyan,
the color of cyan — then, why not,
cyanotic. That seemed effective:
cyanotic aquamarine, aquamarine
with a cyanotic light. But the light
of the cyanotic aquamarine — or
the cyanotic light of the aquamarine — was expanding, along with
the images it evoked, into the story
of my mother, into the prototype
of the Neapolitan mother I was

constructing, violently clashing with her dialectal voice. Was it good, was it bad? I didn't know. I knew only that that little adjective would now make me leave the dull story of a real family and enter into a dark, almost gothic tale. So I retreated in a hurry, but reluctantly. Goodbye "cyanotic." But I had already lost faith: the now true ring, which as a true object of my true experience should have given truth to the writing, seemed inevitably false.

I've lingered on the aquamarine to emphasize that my passion for realism, stubbornly pursued since adolescence, at a certain point became a statement of incapacity. I didn't know how to get an exact reproduction of reality, I wasn't able to tell the thing as it was. I tried a fantasy story, thinking it would be easier, but gave up; I tried neo-avant-garde strategies. But the need to anchor myself in things that had really happened to me or others was indisputably strong. I modeled characters on people I'd known or knew. I noted gestures, ways of speaking, as I saw and heard them. I described landscapes, and the way the light passed over them. I reproduced social dynamics, settings that were economically and culturally far apart. Despite my uneasiness, I let dialect have its space. So I accumulated pages and pages of notes derived from my direct experience.

But I collected only frustrations.

At that point, by chance — which is the case with almost everything, and so also with the books that are truly helpful — I happened to read *Jacques the Fatalist and His Master.* I'm not going to talk about what's important in *Jacques;* I would have to begin with Sterne's *Tristram Shandy,* which precedes and influences it, and I would never end, but, if you haven't read them, believe me, these are books that discuss how difficult it is to tell a story and yet intensify the desire to do it. I will confine myself here to observing that reading *Jacques* enabled me, after many years, to restore to its context the phrase cited by my teacher: "Tell the thing as it is," the master orders Jacques the fatalist. And he answers: "That's not easy. Hasn't a man his own character, his own interests, his own tastes and passions according to which he either exaggerates or understates? Tell the thing as it is, you say! . . . That might not even happen twice in one day in a whole city. And is the person who listens any better qualified to listen than the person who speaks? No. Which is why in a big city it can hardly happen twice in one day that someone's words are understood in the same way as they are spoken." The master replies: "What the devil, Jacques, those principles are enough to outlaw speaking and listening altogether. Say nothing, hear nothing, believe nothing! Just tell the thing as you will, I will listen as I can and believe as I am able."

I had read a lot of books on these subjects, including pointlessly complex passages, and here, plainly expressed, I found some consolation. If every novel I wrote, hefty or slim, turned out to be far from my aspirations — I had boundless ambitions — maybe the reason was not only my incapacity. Telling the real, Jacques emphasized, is constitutionally difficult; you have to deal with the fact that the teller is always a distorting mirror. So? Better to give up? No, the master answers, you don't have to throw everything away: it's arduous to speak truthfully, but you do your best.

A long period began when I tried to do my best. I forced myself to be less exacting than usual, and so, at a certain point, I wrote a book that didn't seem too bad and — this had never happened before — made me want to send it to a publisher. I thought of sending with it a very detailed letter in which I explained how the story had come to me, what real persons and events had nourished it. I tried seriously to write that letter, and went on for many pages. At first it all seemed clear. I brought up the circumstances in which, connecting real events, I had composed the story. Then I went on to describe the real people, the real places that gradually, through deletions and additions, had become the characters and the settings. I moved on to the tradition I was part of, the novels that had inspired me because of the construction of the characters or the orchestration of individual scenes or even the design of a gesture. Finally I reflected on how everything had been distorted, but I defended the distortions as inevitable, considering them, presenting them as a necessary mediation.

And yet the more I immersed myself in the subject, the more complicated the truth of the cover letter became. There was me, me, me. There was my urge to exaggerate defects, minimize virtues, and vice versa. Most important, I glimpsed, I think for the first time, the hazy area of what I could have written in that book but that would have hurt me to write, and so I hadn't done it. Eventually I got tangled up and stopped.

I don't mean that at that point my scribbling found an outlet. Years passed, I read other essential books, I wrote many other unsatisfying things. Yet I would venture to say that, if I made a certain number of small discoveries — somewhat naïve, perhaps, but for me fundamental — I owe it to a milder aesthetic imperative (tell the thing within the limits of the possible) and to that draft of a self-reflective letter.

I'll list some of them.

First small discovery. Until then I had always written in the third person. The first person of that letter, precisely because the more it went on the more tangled it got, and the more tangled it got the more it absorbed me, seemed new and promising.

Second small discovery. I noticed that in literary work reality tended inevitably to be reduced to a rich repertory of tricks that, if skillfully used, gave the impression that the facts had arrived on the page just as they had happened, with all their sociological, political, psychological, ethical, etc., connotations. The opposite, therefore, of the thing as it is. Reality was a game of illusion that to succeed had to pretend that no one had told it, no one had written it, and the real was there, reproduced so well that it made you forget even the marks of the alphabet.

Third small discovery. All narratives were inevitably the work of narrators, male or female, who by nature, by form, could be only a fragment among fragments of reality, whether they were hiding, or presented themselves obliquely, or pretended to be a first-person narrator, or appeared as the author of the entire literary contrivance, with their name on the cover.

Fourth small discovery. Almost without realizing it, from an aspirant to absolute realism I had become a disheartened realist, who now said to herself: I can recount "out there" only if I also recount the me who is "out there" along with all the rest.

Fifth small discovery. Literary work couldn't seriously force the whirlpool of debris that constituted the real into any grammatical or syntactical order.

These were the thoughts that pushed me toward the books I wrote starting in the second half of the nineteen-eighties, and later published. Trying to tell the thing as it is can become paralyzing, I told myself more than thirty years ago. I'm in danger of going deaf, mute, and turning nihilistic thanks to the countless failures and the unpredictability of the rare successes; I will therefore try to tell it as I can, and, who knows, maybe I'll get lucky and tell it as it is. I progressed by trial and error. At first I did this mainly to save from the void the hand that maniacally insisted on wanting to write. But then I became more and more focused. I developed a first-person narrator who, excited by the random collisions between her and the world, deformed the form that she had been laboriously given, and from those dents and distortions and injuries squeezed out other, unsuspected possibilities: all this as she made her way through a story that was increasingly uncontrolled, maybe wasn't even a story but a tangle, in which not only the narrator but the author herself, a pure maker of writing, was enmeshed.

Troubling Love is that: Delia, encased in the features of a cultured woman, tough and autonomous, acts with icy determination within the fixed rules of a small mystery story, until everything — the mystery genre itself — begins to break apart. *The Days of Abandonment* is that: Olga, encased in the features of a cultured woman, a wife and mother, acts with anguished skill within the fixed rules of a small marital crisis, until everything — the "scenes from a marriage" genre itself — begins to break apart. *The Lost Daughter,* especially, is that: Leda, encased in the features of a cultured woman, divorced with grown daughters, acts confidently within the fixed rules of a small horror story, until everything — the horror genre itself — begins to break apart. In these books I muted the idea that I had to describe an "out there" arranged in a narrative order and, without letting it show, had the duty to record it on the great scroll of realistic literature. Instead, I dipped into the warehouse of literary expression, taking out what I needed — different genres, different techniques, effects, and, why not, unpleasant effects — without indicating boundaries between high and low. I moved on not to a narrative voice — no voice, no imitation of voices — but to a female first person who is all writing and, writing, tells how, in certain circumstances, deviations, unexpected jolts, erratic leaps occurred, which had been able to upset the solidity of the chessboard on which she was castled.

I'd like to emphasize this last point. Imagining Delia, Olga, and Leda as first persons who narrate in writing — what is before the reader's eyes is *their* writing — was important for me. It also allowed me to imagine — I purposely insist on this verb — the me who writes not as a woman who among her many other activities makes literature but as an exclusively literary work, an author who, creating the writing of Delia, Olga, and Leda, creates herself. It seemed to me that I could thus trace a perimeter of freedom, within which I could display, without self-censure, capacity and incapacity, virtues and flaws, wounds that don't heal and sutures, obscure feelings and emotions. Not only that: it also seemed to me that I could produce that double writing I was talking about. I tried, that is, to calibrate the two kinds of writing, using the more compliant for a slow fake-realist pace and the more unruly to break down with its fiction the fiction of the first.

In those three books I begin with an integrating type of writing, based on consistency, which establishes a world with all its scaffolding in the right place. It's a solid cage: I construct it using the necessary facts of reality, hidden citations from ancient and modern myths, the trove of my reading. Then comes — or at least I count on its coming — the convulsive, disintegrating type of writing, which produces oxymorons, ugly-beautiful, beautiful-ugly, and spreads inconsistencies and contradictions. It carries the past in the present and the present in the past, it confuses the bodies of mother and daughter, overturns established roles, transforms the poison of female suffering into a real poison that involves animals, confuses them with humans and kills them, changes a normally functioning door into a door that no longer opens and then does, makes threatening or suffering or lethal or salvific trees, cicadas, a rough sea, hatpins, dolls, beach worms.

Both kinds of writing are mine and, at the same time, Delia's, Olga's, Leda's. I write people, places, times, but in words that have been inspired in me by people, places, times, in a dizzying mixture of creators with created, of forms with forms. That is, this writing is the always random result of how Delia, Olga, and Leda are recorded in the registry office of fictions, and of how I, the author — a fiction forever incomplete, molded by years and years of reading and the desire to write — invent and disrupt the writing that has recorded them. I am, I would say, their auto-biography as they are mine.

Here, to end for the moment the discussion of the little I seem to know of those first three books, I should add that Delia, Olga, and Leda are imagined as women who, because of the events of their lives, have become tightly sealed bodies. In the past they have laid down bridges from themselves toward the other, but they haven't been successful, and have remained alone. They don't have ongoing relations with relatives, they don't have women friends, they don't trust themselves and don't entrust themselves to husbands, lovers, or even children. We don't know what they're like physically, because no

one describes them. Most important, they are the sole source of the
story. There is no way to compare
their version of the facts with others' versions. Besides, they seem to
have come so close to the facts of
their story that they don't have a
view of the whole, don't truly know
the meaning of what they say. I
wanted them like that. Writing, I
rejected conventional distancing.
Where they eliminated the distance
from their wounds, I eliminated the
distance from their suffering. And I
confused myself, the author, with
the version they gave of the story,
and with their isolated situation, so
that even I who was writing avoided
the role of the other, the external,
she who witnesses what really hap-

pened.

In *Troubling Love* and in *The Days of Abandonment* this self-imprisonment was a conscious aesthetic choice. For example, neither Delia nor I knows what happened to Delia's mother on the beach; for example, neither Olga nor I knows why the door of the apartment suddenly won't open and suddenly opens. I can, like Delia, like Olga, construct hypotheses, and like them I have to be content with those, we have no way of verifying them.

The Lost Daughter is, programmatically, more radical. Leda carries out an act — stealing the doll — that she is unable to give meaning to, either at the beginning of her story or at the end. And I myself, Elena Ferrante, conceived my writing and hers in such a way that in both of us the absolute, concentrated isolation of the narrative discourse would reach a point of no return. We are both simply driven to exhaustion, summarized in Leda's final remark, to her daughters: "I'm dead, but I'm fine."

For some years I considered *The Lost Daughter* a final book, or anyway the last that I would publish. My adolescent mania for realism was spent. Only a desire for truth remained which made me reject reportorial naturalism, with its splashes of dialect, the fine writing that sugarcoats the pill, the female characters always ready to lift up their heads and win. My women, because I could see only one way that adequately and truthfully described them and myself, ended up, against my will — I insist: you don't tell the story without the shoves of others; that old principle has remained firm — in a sort of solipsism, without which, however, I saw, for me as an author, only a regression toward the inauthentic.

Then, completely by chance, I returned to a book, published by Feltrinelli, that I had read when it came out, in 1997 or 1998: *Tu che mi guardi, tu che mi racconti* (published in English in 2000 as *Relating Narratives: Storytelling and*

Selfhood), by Adriana Cavarero. That first reading hadn't been helpful to me, in fact it had weakened my faith in the path I had started on with *Troubling Love,* even though I found its analysis of both the female impulse to narrate oneself and the desire to be narrated fascinating. Or at least that's how I remember it. However, it's not that first reading I want to talk about but the second.

I was trying to get out of the dead end of *The Lost Daughter* by drafting a new story of mothers and daughters — a crowded, expansive story, that, in my intention, would span some seventy years — when I picked up Cavarero's book again. It seemed new, a book I had never read, starting from the use she makes of Karen Blixen and the story of the stork, recounted in *Out of Africa*. But what kindled my imagination was an expression: *the necessary other*. It serves as the title of an entire chapter, is set up by a complex dialogue with Hannah Arendt, skirts the theme of narcissism, and arrives, finally, at the following definition:

> The necessary other is . . . a finitude that remains irremediably an other in all the fragile and unjudgeable insubstitutability of her existing.
>
> (Translated by Paul A. Kottman)

It was, I recall, a shock. *An other* seemed to me what I needed in order to leave the three earlier books and yet stay within them.

But I want to proceed in order. Among the many books Cavarero used to advance her argument, she cited, at a certain point, *Non credere di avere dei diritti* (published in English as *Sexual Difference: A Theory of Social-Symbolic Practice*), an extremely important Italian feminist text, published by the Milan Women's Bookstore Collective. From it she extrapolated a brief story of friendship. It was an encounter between two women, Emilia and Amalia, against the background of the 1970s and the "150 hours," a union victory giving workers the right to a hundred and fifty hours of courses, or similar activities, that furthered their personal development. Amalia is an excellent natural storyteller, and at first she finds Emilia boring, because she always says the same things. But then, as they read each other's exercises for the course, Amalia becomes more attentive, and more interested in Emilia's fragments of writing. And since Emilia admires Amalia's writing to the point where it makes her weep, Amalia has the urge to write the facts of her friend's life and to make her a gift of the text: a gift that Emilia, overcome by emotion, will carry forever in her purse.

I had read *Sexual Difference* many years earlier and hadn't really noticed Emilia and Amalia. But Cavarero extracted those pale figures of women from the two pages or so that concerned them and spoke about them with great sensitivity and intelligence. She wrote about the "narrative character of female friendships." She wrote — listen to this — about "the intersection of autobiographical narrations that insure the result of the reciprocal biographical activity." She wrote: "At work . . . is a mechanism of reciprocity through which the narratable self of each woman passes to auto-narration so that the other may know a story that she can in turn tell others, certainly, but, most important, again tells the woman who is its protagonist." She summarized: "Put simply, I tell you my story in order to make you tell it to me." I was enthusiastic. It was what I — not putting it simply — was trying to write in my draft of an endless novel centered on two women friends who weave together the stories of their experience, in a less edifying manner than Emilia and Amalia.

I picked up *Sexual Difference* again. The pages where Emilia and Amalia figured became important to the story I was drafting. I even found a passage that Cavarero hadn't quoted directly, but that fired my imagination. Amalia, the good writer, at a certain point says of Emilia: "This woman truly understood things: she wrote a lot of sentences that were disconnected but very true and profound." I immediately liked that "truly." I liked that "true and profound." I felt that Amalia, who loved to write and knew she was good at it, had an uncontainable admiration for Emilia's attempts to write. It seemed to me that I could even perceive a feeling like envy in the face of a result that, though she was good, Amalia knew she couldn't achieve.

I began to exaggerate, as I typically do. Cavarero writes: "We do not come to know the adored pages that Emilia preserves in her handbag." But she doesn't regret either the loss of Amalia's text or the loss of Emilia's fragments, which she calls "awkward autobiographical attempts." With good reason: she intends her investigation to accentuate the positive effects of the narrative friendship between two women; she isn't worried about the dynamics between the texts. Whereas I regretted not having those texts: I felt that they were close to my problems as a narrator, because I knew what diligent writing was and what writing that goes over the margins was. And I imagined — I thought — that if I had at least Amalia's text I would be able to discern Emilia's true and profound sentences rising up in it. I'm almost positive that the dynamic between Elena's writing and Lila's came to me from those thoughts. In fact I'd only had to read Amalia's admiring words and right away, I confess, her friend's "disconnected sentences" had become "true writing," the writing that bursts in (Dante would have described it: "almost as if it moved of its own accord") and ends up beautifully enclosed between the red lines of a notebook. In other words, I imagined that Amalia, with her ability to write, had tamed Emilia's fragments, and that Emilia, the necessary other, was happy precisely about that taming.

Cavarero, I must say at this point, doesn't use that term in relation to Emilia: she uses it about Alice B. Toklas, the person whose autobiography — note: autobiography, not biography — is written by Gertrude Stein. All right: decades earlier, I had utterly misread *The Autobiography of Alice B. Toklas.* I reread it, in the phase when I was writing my long draft, taking off from the pages that Adriana Cavarero devoted to it. And I would like to say that I had understood nothing: *The Autobiography of Alice B. Toklas* is a great book, in structure, in execution. I will copy some of Cavarero's passages which inspired me to look at it again:

The autobiographical and biographical genres are superimposed upon one another . . . Gertrude writes her own life story making it told by another: by Alice, her friend and partner, her lover . . . The gigantic egotism of Gertrude Stein succeeds in thus producing a literary fiction of stories that intersect where she herself stands out and where Alice — the lover, the friend — still appears as the other who watches her and as the other who tells her story.

It's probably starting here that the relationship between Lenù and Lila, and between their writing, became clearer to me. And it's probably starting here that I began to think that I could leave Olga, Delia, and especially Leda by working on a sort of mutual necessary otherness, describing, that is, a bond between two people merged with one another but not reducible to one another.

Rereading the *Autobiography* sent me even farther in that direction. It seemed to me that the book had turned out so well because in the writing — and maybe also in reality — Gertrude's egotism, as Cavarero calls it, is satisfied through a double function: that of the author, Gertrude Stein, who signs the work, and that of the character to whom the author gives her own name, printed on the cover, Gertrude Stein. But note: if you read or reread the book, follow the development, line by line, of Alice Toklas. In her guise as first-person narrator, she takes the lead, emerging in full relief. Not coincidentally, in the splendid final passage, when, with Alice unable to make up her mind, Gertrude promises to write her friend's autobiography, the promise is formulated like this: "I am going to write it as simply as Defoe did the autobiography of Robinson Crusoe." That is, I will write about you, my dear friend-lover-wife, in the only possible way one can write the autobiography of someone else: by making it a first-person fiction, you the first-person protagonist, a Robinson, not a Friday. Besides, although Alice is a wife, and assigned to write about the wives of geniuses, how, within the structure of the text and without the necessary literary stature, could she recognize and represent with true ability not only the wives of geniuses — which among other things she does very well — but a genius wife, Gertrude, described in the third person amid genius males?

In this connection I want to end by citing a famous passage in which Alice writes about meeting Gertrude for the first time:

> I was impressed by the coral brooch she wore and by her voice. I may say that only three times in my life have I met a genius and each time a bell within me rang and I was not mistaken, and I may say in each case it was before there was any general

recognition of the quality of genius in them. The three geniuses of whom I wish to speak are Gertrude Stein, Pablo Picasso and Alfred Whitehead.

I would point out here only one thing. I found it amazing that a woman, the woman who was on the cover, boldly defines herself, through the mouth of her "necessary other," as a genius and, setting herself beside two men, puts herself first. She seemed to have an incomparable immodesty, and I felt like laughing, a laugh of sympathy. I can't swear to it, but I think it was then that, after having for a certain period called my draft *The Necessary Friend,* I began calling it *My*

Brilliant Friend — in the Italian *L'amica geniale.* But I will return to this next time.

■ ■ ■ ■

Histories, I

■ ■ ■ ■

Ladies and gentlemen, I will begin this final meeting with a short poem by Emily Dickinson, about history and witches, in order to pick up the discussion of last time, when I was talking about the Neapolitan Novels and writing that inspires and activates other writing. It's just a few lines:

Witchcraft was hung, in History,
But History and I
Find all the Witchcraft that we

need

Around us, every Day —

What I've always liked about this handful of words is the "and" that proudly unites "History and I." In the first line is the written account we call History, which has hung witchcraft on the gallows. In the three other lines, introduced by an adversative "but," is the "I," the "I" that unites with the story of the past and thus, every day, thanks to that union with History, finds, around itself, all the witchcraft it needs.

I read the poem more or less like that for some decades, and the reference to the witches made me fantasize excitedly that, from the writing that suffocated the spells, a female "I" would derive a writing that, as needed, would return to complete them in daily life, joining people and things that supposedly couldn't be joined. Thus, among the suggestions that led me to the Neapolitan Novels, I must surely add the image that those lines have always evoked for me: a woman who sits at a table and writes "History and I" as a challenge, almost a confrontation, and with that juxtaposition gives a furious start to a thread of words that from the hostile writing of the witches' art extracts a story that draws on that art. Over time, I think, I gave that figure of a woman a modern posture when I saw her, brow furrowed, gaze intense, writing on the computer in an apartment in Turin, trying to invent other women, mothers, sisters, friends — a witch friend — and places in Naples, and small ordeals and sufferings of relatives and acquaintances, and the past sixty years of History, appropriating them from the many texts that had already put them in writing. I felt she was true, with a truth that had to do with me.

Before I go on, let me return to Gertrude Stein and *The Autobiography of Alice B. Toklas.* I'd like to take from it a few more things that are important to me on the theme of writing that's inspired by other writing and, if it goes well, finds its truth.

The "genuine 'real life,'" as Dostoyevsky called it, is an obsession, a torment for the writer. With greater or less ability we fabricate fictions not so that the false will seem true but to tell the most unspeakable truth with absolute faithfulness through the fiction. In that book Gertrude Stein called Hemingway a coward: "yellow," she said. And she said it because in her opinion Ernest, rather than telling the story of the true Hemingway, about whom he would certainly have written a great work, confined himself to "confessions" — so she called them — comfortable confessions, confessions that, she insisted, were good for advancing his career.

Let's leave aside the art of saying mean things in a good-humored tone, which is also plentiful in the *Autobiography.* In substance Stein's charge is not: Hemingway tries to tell the truth but presents false confessions. The charge is: Hemingway, who could use his talent to write about his real self, offers us a literary product that is well made, successful, but false for opportunistic reasons. At this point the next question has to be: if Hemingway, who could effectively write the story of the real Ernest, fabricates only "confessions" that are useful for his career, what does Stein do in order not to tar herself with the same brush and to write about the real Gertrude?

I'll tell you my idea. Stein doesn't confine herself to writing about her own existence in the world, keeping within an easily manageable literary form, which she calls, a little brusquely, "confession." Nor does she confine herself, as she knows very well how to do, to establishing a style; that is, imposing her own tonality on words and phrases. But she takes a highly structured genre like autobiography and deforms it. That is her differentness, and maybe Dickinson would say: that is her skill as a witch. She introduces the personal information of Alice and herself and others, the biographical material of Alice and herself and others, not into an easily manageable liter-

117

ary form but into the fiction of an easily manageable literary form, and therefore a form that, precisely because it's false, can and must be deformed.

Just think about what you find on the cover of *The Autobiography of Alice B. Toklas.* There, apparently, is an ironic reference to the effects of truth that the book originally intended, pretending to offer readers not made-up stories but true accounts of journeys to the underworld, true rediscovered manuscripts, true letters, true diaries. That is, if Gertrude Stein were continuing to apply the old form, she would have to present as true the invented autobiography of some character of her creation. Instead

the form receives a blow that deforms it. Gertrude Stein, a real
person, calls herself the author —
author — of an autobiography written by Alice Toklas, a person not
invented but real, in which the
autobiographical "I" talks largely
not about herself but about someone else, that is, Gertrude Stein, a
brilliant real person.

Some will say that it is, therefore,
merely a "bizarre subterfuge." But
that's an ungenerous reductivism.
Stein is, rather, demonstrating that
writing about the true Gertrude
isn't simply a matter of writing
truthfully but involves applying
force to the great containers of
literary writing, to the forms that
at the moment seem most comfort-

able, most beautiful, and instead are a death trap for our intention to write "truthfully." To do this, she treats the "I" that is writing about itself — Alice B. Toklas, the source of the biographical truth — as a fiction, as a woman whose "life and opinions" must be written about in the form of autobiography, as a Huckleberry Finn is written by the pen of Mark Twain. But, having done that, she inserts a dizzying, disruptive element of fiction, which comes from the true Alice. Toklas is the real typist of Stein's texts, she helps correct the proofs. She is therefore — as she says in the text — the reader who knows Stein's writing most thoroughly. And, indeed, in the fiction she continuously gives the impression that she's correcting, adding, clarifying, annotating, to the point where the fake autobiography seems like a text that the two women have in fact written, one beside the other, one dictating, the other at the typewriter, pausing, remembering, reflecting.

This is what upends the traditional relations between invented story, autobiographical truth, and biographical truth, making Stein's book a great lesson for the "I" who wants to write, surely a more stimulating lesson, today, than what we might get from Hemingway's books. Ernest's mistake is to succeed by prudently respecting the rules of an old, well-known game;

Gertrude's virtue is to succeed by sticking to the old, well-known game but in order to disrupt it and bend it to her purposes.

Naturally the Stein-Hemingway question has within it a substantial problem: cowardice or not, career or not, writing with truth is really difficult, perhaps impossible. In *Notes from Underground,* Dostoyevsky has his terrible protagonist say:

> We've become so estranged that at times we feel some kind of revulsion for genuine "real life," and therefore we can't bear to be reminded of it. Why, we've reached a point where we almost regard "real life" as hard work, as

a job, and we've all agreed in private that it's really better in books.

(Translated by Michael Katz)

Anyone who has literary ambitions knows that the motivations, both great and small, that impel the hand to write come from "real life": the yearning to describe the pain of love, the pain of living, the anguish of death; the need to straighten the world that is all crooked; the search for a new morality that will reshape us; the urgency to give voice to the humble, to strip away power and its atrocities; the need to prophesy disasters but also to design happy worlds to come from there. One morning something may shift inside me, maybe just a wrong that was done to my mother, and the "I" looks out, dying to write, and I start putting down the first lines of a story. Immediately a long tradition made up of others' stories crowds around, stories that have moved or angered me, that resemble mine, not to mention the language of books, newspapers, films, television, songs, or a pile of tricks good for pushing "real life" into writing — all things that I learned almost without noticing. It's natural for me to insert my confused experience into that collection of formulas. And it's a great moment. If I'm lucky, if I have some talent, sentences arrive that seem to say what I want to say just as it should be said. Then I can tell myself proudly: that's my voice, with my voice I am describing my real life. And others will say it to me, too, and I'll look for that cadence of mine every time, and if it doesn't appear I'll be afraid I've lost it, and if it does appear I'll be afraid of using it up.

You hear? My, my, my. How often we repeat that possessive adjective. In fact, a first big step forward, in the matter of writing, is to discover exactly the opposite: that what we triumphantly consider ours belongs to others. Dealings with the world, yes, at any time they are entirely ours. But the words — the written form in which we enclose them, attentive to the red margins of our notebooks — are not. We have to accept the fact that no word is truly ours. We have to give up the idea that writing miraculously releases a voice of our own, a tonality of our own: in my view that is a lazy way of talking about writing. Writing is, rather, entering an immense cemetery where every tomb is waiting to be profaned. Writing is getting comfortable with everything that has already been written — great literature and commercial literature, if useful, the novel-essay and the screenplay — and in turn becoming, within the limits of one's own dizzying, crowded individuality, something written. Writing is seizing everything that has already been written and gradually learning to spend that enormous fortune. We mustn't let ourselves be flattered by those who say: here's someone who has a tonality of her own. Everything, in writing, has a long history behind it. Even my uprising, my spilling over the margins, my yearning is part of an eruption that came before me and goes beyond me. Thus when I talk about my "I" who writes, I should immediately add that I'm talking about my "I" who has read (even when it's a question of distracted reading, the trickiest kind of reading). And I should emphasize that every book read carries within itself a host of other writings that, consciously or inadvertently, I've taken in. That is, writing about our own joys and wounds and sense of the world means writing in every way, always, knowing that we are the product, good or bad, of encounters and clashes, sought out and accidental, with the stuff of others. The most serious error of the "I" who writes, the most serious naiveté, is the Robinsonian: imagining oneself, that is, as a Robinson who is smug about his life on the desert island, pretending that all the odds and ends he carried off the ship haven't contributed to his success; or like a Homer who doesn't confess to himself that he's working on materials that have been elaborated and transmitted orally. We don't do that, but we remake "real life." And as soon as we realize it, then, if we're not cowards, we search desperately for a way to tell the genuine "real life."

Thus writing is a cage and we enter it right away, with our first line. It's a problem that has been confronted with suffering, I would say with anguish, precisely by those who have worked with the most dedication and engagement. Ingeborg Bachmann, for example, insisted all her life on the effort to "speak truly." In her Frankfurt lectures, 1959–60, she speaks of the plurality of the "I" who writes — the fourth lecture is entitled just that: *The I Who Writes* — and of the permanent risk of falsehood, in a

way that for those who love literature is still needed today. A rule
that was important for me figures
in her fifth lecture:

> We have to work hard with the
> bad language that we have inher-
> ited to arrive at that language
> which has never yet ruled, but
> which rules our intuition, and
> which we imitate.

I would place the emphasis there:
we have to work hard with the bad
language. I would emphasize it
before offering another citation,
from a 1955 interview, that struck
me and that I've often found useful, adapting it, as I have many passages of Bachmann's. The inter-
viewer is asking her about the

complicated, abstract language of contemporary poetry, and she says:

I believe that old images, like Mörike's or Goethe's, can no longer be used, that they shouldn't be used anymore, because in our mouths they would sound false. We have to find true sentences, which correspond to the condition of our conscience and to this changed world.

You see: there's the pressure of the changed world; there's the conscience that records its sins; there's a language that asks for power; there's the "I" who writes, who intuits the language and tries to change that intuition into true sentences. But the fact is that we can't set aside the old images, the bad language. They're right in front of us, they exist. Where will we get new images, good language? Our writing has to work on the writing that exists — false in our mouths even if it's Mörike's, Goethe's — if it wants to get what's not there yet. Work how, though? Let's look at one last passage from Bachmann's first Frankfurt lecture:

> Moreover quality can now and then be found in an average person's poem, in a good short story, in an attractive, clever novel; it is not in short supply; there is certainly no lack of experts, even today, and there are flukes, or oddities, or deviant productions

on the fringes that can become personal favorites of ours. And yet only a trajectory, a continuous manifestation, a mathematical constant, an unmistakable world of words, a world of characters, and a world of conflicts, can prompt us to see a writer as inevitable.

It's true, tragically true. Any of us can do something good, in writing, when the world gives us a shove, but a true writer is inevitable only when we recognize in the work a unique and unmistakable universe of words, figures, conflicts. Yet where and how that well-made true universe has been established and developed, using the bad language and the inherited false words, well, it remains difficult to say. Over the years, I've often changed my idea. But I've never stopped believing in the importance of the writing we've inherited, which the "I" who writes, like it or not, is made of. Nor have I ever underestimated the chance occurrence that sets off the hand that writes, when it goes fishing for gifts in the "bad language." Like Bachmann, I think it's right to make a distinction between a beautiful poem, a good story, an attractive, clever novel by an average person and the work of one who is inevitably an author. It's a distinction that's fundamental for the fate of literature. But I tend to imagine, first, that the ordinary person and

the extraordinary person set off
from the same terrain: literary writing with its cathedrals, its country
parishes, its tabernacles in dark al-
leys; and, second, that chance —
the hand that rummages in the
bran pie and pulls out words —
plays the same role in both the
minor work and the great work.
True sentences, good or epochal,
always seek a path of their own
within clichés. And clichés were
once true sentences that dug a way
out among clichés. In this chain of
works great and small, in every link
large or small, there is hard work
and accidental illuminations, effort
and luck. The road to Damascus
isn't as well marked as the road
dedicated to revelation. It's a road

like any other on which, slogging and sweating, we may by chance become aware of another possible way.

Thus in order to devote ourselves to literary work must we subscribe to the great scroll of writing? Yes. Writing inevitably has to reckon with other writing, and it's from the terrain of the already written that the sentence might jump out that sets in motion a small admirable book or the great book that displays a trajectory and constructs a unique world of words, characters, and conflicts.

If that's true for the male "I" who writes, it's even more so for the female. A woman who wants to write has unavoidably to deal not only with the entire literary patrimony she's been brought up on and in virtue of which she wants to and can express herself but with the fact that that patrimony is essentially male and by its nature doesn't provide true female sentences. Since I was six my "I" made of writing has consumed writing mostly by men, considering it universal, and my own scribbling comes from it. Not only that. This female "I" brought up on male writing also has had to incorporate a kind of writing by women for women that belonged to it, was appropriate to it — writing in itself minor precisely because it was barely known by men, and considered by them something for women, that is, inessential. I've known in my life very cultured men who not only had never read Elsa Morante or Natalia Ginzburg or Anna Maria Ortese but had never read Jane Austen, the Brontë sisters, Virginia Woolf. And I myself, as a girl, wished to avoid as far as possible writing by women: I felt I had different ambitions.

I mean that our "I" — the female "I" who writes — has had an arduous journey; she is still finding her way and will go on doing so indefinitely. As soon as we try to write something, one more problem regarding the inadequacy of the writing is added to those I've tried to list: that not a single page, whether polished or rough, speaks our truth as women completely, in fact often doesn't speak it at all. We notice an excess leaking out, for which a special container is needed, but if it goes well we manage to find only one that is compatible. Here is a poem by the Mexican poet María Guerra:

I lost a poem.
Already written
And ready on the page
To put in the form of a book
I looked in vain.
It was a poem
With a vocation for wind.

This is precisely what happens to our efforts to write: the words are ready *para formar el libro,* says María Guerra, and yet they won't stay in the form, they overflow the margins, get lost in the wind.

As a child it seemed to me that that's how things were. As a child I felt excessive, I went too far. It wasn't only a question of writing. Speech, too, was obliged to stay shut up in women's conversations; or in the sentences considered speakable, with the proper female tonality, in dialogue with males; or in the words that were obscenely theirs and that we said laughing but also disgusted. The rest was silent, we could never express ourselves fully. We drew on spoken Italian in the false speech of radio and television, but that was no good. Dialect didn't help, either. There was always something that didn't work, that made us uneasy.

I've had problems with dialect; I've never managed to convince myself that it allowed more truth than written Italian. Italo Svevo, who through Zeno Cosini considered every confession written in Tuscan Italian a lie, believed that things turned out better for him in the Triestine dialect. For a long time I, too, believed that about Neapolitan, and worked on it a lot. I love my city, and it seemed to me that Naples couldn't be written about without its language. Significant passages of *Troubling Love* and even of the Neapolitan Novels were written in dialect, but in the end I

either eliminated them or transformed them into an Italian with a
Neapolitan cadence. This is because dialectal vocabulary and
syntax, as soon as they're written,
seem even more false than Italian.
The transcription should give an
effective imitation of speech; and
instead, to my ear, it seems a betrayal. Once written, besides, Neapolitan seems sterilized. It loses
passion, loses affect, loses the sense
of danger it often communicated
to me. In my childhood and adolescence it was the language of coarse
male vulgarity, the language of the
violence of men calling to you on
the street, or, contrarily, the sugary-
sweet language with which women
were taken in. My emotion, natu-

rally, part of my personal experiences. Gradually, I began to find it could be effective in a literary work, not used as it typically is in the realist tale but as a subterranean stream, a cadence within the language, a caption, a disturbance in the writing that suddenly erupts with a few, usually obscene words.

The challenge, I thought and think, is to learn to use with freedom the cage we're shut up in. It's a painful contradiction: how can one use a cage with freedom, whether it's a solid literary genre or established expressive habits or even the language itself, dialect? A possible answer seemed to me Stein's: adapting and at the same time deforming. Maintain distance:

yes, but only to then get as close as possible. Avoid the pure outburst? Yes, but then burst out. Aim at consistency? Yes, but then be inconsistent. Make a polished, highly polished, draft, until the words no longer encounter friction with the meanings? Yes, but then leave it rough. Overload the genres with conventional expectations? Yes, but in order to disappoint them. That is, inhabit the forms and then deform everything that doesn't contain us entirely, that can't in any way contain us. It seemed to me effective for the ornate lies of the great literary catalogue to show lumps and cracks, to bang against one another. I hoped that an unexpected truth would emerge, surprising me above all.

That is how I worked, especially with the most recent books I've published, the Neapolitan Novels and *The Lying Life of Adults.* I don't know if they're successful or not, I don't know that about any of my books. But I do know that, much more than the first three, they have at their center the act of telling the story and telling the story of women's lives. In the other books the protagonists were writing for themselves; they were writing autobiographies, diaries, confessions, driven by hidden wounds. Now that the first-person narrator has friends, the work is not to write for herself about dealings with the world but to write about the others, to be written about by them, in a complex interplay of identification and estrangement.

In the Neapolitan Novels, I intended the story of the writing — of Elena's writing, of Lila's writing, and in fact that of the author herself — to be the thread that holds together the entire encounter-clash between the two friends and, with it, the fiction of the world, of the epoch within which they act. I took that trajectory because I'd become convinced in recent years that every narrative should include, within itself, the adventure of its writing, what gives it form. As a result I tried to tell a story structurally based on the fact that ever since they were children the two protagonists have tried to subjugate the hostile world around them through reading and writing. They buy the first book in their lives with the dirty money of a camorrist. They read it together and plan to write a book together to become rich and powerful. But Lila breaks the pact and writes a child's book by herself, whose writing so impresses Lenù that for the rest of her life she is driven to try to contain it in her own.

I've already spoken about the two kinds of writing I know — diligent writing and writing that goes beyond boundaries — and still have no control over. I've talked about suggestions derived from Cavarero, from Emilia and Amalia, from Toklas and Stein, from Dickinson, from Bachmann. All this — and other things that I don't have time to discuss — contributed to the creation of Lenù, who wants to contain Lila's convulsive talent in her diligence, and Lila, who prods her friend, molds her existence, claims from her more and more.

The "I" who writes and publishes is Lenù's. Throughout the Neapolitan Novels, we never know anything of Lila's extraordinary writing except what Lenù summarizes for us, or the little that emerges in Lenù's writing. I said to myself at a certain point: you should make up some passages from Lila's letters or notebooks. But it seemed to me inconsistent with Lenù's rebellious inferiority, with her deluded autonomy that aims, in a process as complex as it is contradictory, at absorbing Lila by taking away her power, and empowering Lila by absorbing her. And, besides — I confessed when the book was going well — would I who write along with Lenù, I, the author, even be able to create Lila's writing? Am I not inventing that extraordinary writing just to describe the inadequacy of my own?

During one phase of drafting the story, I developed the idea that Lila entered Lenù's computer and improved the text, mixing her way of writing with her friend's. I wrote many pages in which Elena's diligent writing changed, was fused, confused with Lila's uncontrollable writing. But those attempts seemed artificial and in essence incongruous: I left only a few traces of that possible development. Especially since, if I had taken that direction, it would have meant that, progressively changing Lenù's writing into collaborative writing with Lila's, I would have had to decisively change the overall design of the narrative. It would have meant that, once Lila had broken the pact of writing a book together with Lenù, Lenù, when it came to writing, would have been unable to write anything but a randomly successful novel, like Hemingway's books for Stein, like the books by the average people Bachmann cites, those, that is, who make a career but no more. Lenù, on the level of writing, had to be fulfilled but without true satisfaction. She knows that Lila doesn't like her books. She knows that, writing, she puts her friend's writing in the margins. She knows that by herself she will never get past the bad language, the old images that ring false, while her friend probably has. Inserting into this structure a fusion of the two kinds of writing, a confusion, meant reaching a happy ending in which what the two girls hadn't done — write a book together — they did now as adults in a sort of final book that is the story of their lives. Impossible, for me. While I was writing the Neapolitan Novels, an ending like that was inconceivable.

Something changed recently. While I was planning *The Lying Life of Adults* I thought again of the Dickinson poem that I cited at the beginning of today's talk, and only then, after all this time, became aware of an important moment. Let's hear it again:

Witchcraft was hung, in History,
But History and I
Find all the Witchcraft that we
    need
Around us, every Day —

What had I not paid attention to? I hadn't paid attention to how "History and I" generated an "us" and a space "around us." Although the Neapolitan quartet had been motivated by those lines, it wasn't successful. In the tumult of History, in the crowd of female characters with their stories, the narrative thread, so as not to risk breaking, held on to the *you and I.* Of course, in relation to the sealed "I" of the three preceding books, the reciprocal *inleiarsi,* or entering into each other (a Dantesque word, even if Dante didn't invent it), of Lila and Lenù was a giant step.

But now, in my view, a new limit emerged. The original sin of the two friends was to believe they could do it on their own, the former as a child, the latter as an adult. They are encapsulated in the distinction between those who from the bad language create only small books and those who instead are able to write inevitable books: Lenù who ends up with the meagerness and perishability of her own works, recognized by her daughters among others, and Lila who avoids any publication, giving herself a permanent escape.

With *The Lying Life* I tried to do something else. I conceived a story in which you don't know who the woman-character writing is. It could be any of those who appear in the story, and could pretend to be the "I" of Giovanna, starting, of course, with Giovanna herself. The story was to be very long, to oscillate perpetually between lie and truth, with a comprehensive title that summed up the condition of a majority of the female characters: *widowhood.* I myself, in my function as author, was to enter the scene, describing my difficulties in writing and the effort of holding together different sources, incoherent narrative segments, sensibilities that were similar yet in conflict, very different qualities of writing. But already with the first endless draft my strength failed. The undertaking seemed to me fated to remain incomplete, more a tangle than a story. I rule out, at the moment, going beyond the volume-preamble I've published, and, besides, it seems to me that that book can manage on its own.

■ ■ ■ ■

I now think that if literature written by women wants to have its own writing of truth, the work of each of us is needed. For a long span of time we'll have to give up the distinction between those who make only average books and those who create inevitable verbal universes. Against the bad language that historically doesn't provide a welcome for our truth, we have to confuse, fuse our talents, not a line should be lost in the wind. We can do it. And in connection with this, I'd like to reflect yet again on the Dickinson poem that so far today has guided us:

Witchcraft was hung, in History,
But History and I
Find all the Witchcraft that we
   need
Around us, every Day —

I believe that the pure and simple joining of the female "I" to History changes History. The History of the first line, the one that hangs the witch's work on the gallows — note, something important has happened — is not, can no longer be, the History of the second, the one with which we find, around us, all the witchcraft we need.

■ ■ ■ ■

DANTE'S RIB

■ ■ ■ ■

In a 1966 essay, Maria Corti — to whose extraordinary work I owe the impulse to reread Dante after first reading him in high school — drew a distinction, with proper sarcasm, between Eugenio Montale's competence on Dantean matters and "a certain dilettantism, although brilliant, in vogue among our writers, or vacuum of militant improvisation, [which] gets accustomed to rapidly ransacking a text or two and then produces, confident in its own cultural virginity." I agree with each of those words. So then why did I decide to confirm here, on this occasion, what Corti, fifty-five years ago, said of so many of us who have given in to the urge to scribble?

Out of love, I would say. Rather, out of love as it became fixed in my mind for the first time when, as a teenager, I was reading the poems of Dante and his friends: love associated with fear, trembling, even anguish and horror. I got the impression, at the age of sixteen, that love was suffering, exposing oneself to certain danger. And not so much because death was always around the corner but because of the very nature of love, because of an energy it had that heightened and at the same time stunned and humiliated the spirit of life. Meanwhile, however, deeply etched in me was the notion that without love it was impossible to greet others, and thus save ourselves, in heaven as on earth, since exposing oneself, risk, was inevitable. I started writing this essay first of all to admit to myself that I loved and love Dante's words but am exhausted by their force; and that simply trying to get to the bottom of this love — without, among other things, the assiduous study that Corti justly insists on — frightens me. As a result I've decided to stick to the two or three things that I took from Dante, in high school and university — when I wanted more than anything else to write — and that later, amid countless adjustments and misunderstandings, I nurtured in my mind as if they were mine.

The Dante I read and studied, fifty years ago, started from the Provençal and Siculo-Tuscan tradition; extracted from that a new style of his own, interpreting almost without intending to the need of the city's ruling class for a more refined literature; devoted himself to study, becoming for all practical purposes a wise poet-philosopher who put Christ at the center of human history; and, finally, constructed the prodigious edifice of the Commedia based on an Aristotelian rationalism very slightly veined, in the last canticle, with mysticism.

This formula I memorized diligently at the time, and, if necessary, I readily use it again today, with some updating. But if I had to name what really struck me as a teenager — and not so much as a student but as a fledgling reader and aspiring writer — I would start with the discovery that Dante describes the act of writing obsessively, literally and figuratively, constantly presenting its power and its inadequacy, and the provisional nature of success and failure.

I was disturbed in particular by the representation of failure. It seemed to me that even when Dante emphasized his successes, he couldn't avoid the idea that encasing human experience in the alphabet is an art susceptible to searing disappointments. I'm not about to bore you here with the numerous citations I found in my notebooks of the time. I will say only that even when I first read Dante in high school, I felt great pity for Bonagiunta. The words that Dante puts in his mouth, in Canto 24 of Purgatory, moved me.

"O frate, issa vegg'io", diss'elli, "il nodo che 'l Notaro e Guittone e me ritenne di qua dal dolce stil novo ch'i' odo! Io veggio ben come le vostre penne di retro al dittator sen vanno strette, che de le nostre certo non avvenne; e qual più a gradire oltre si mette, non vede più da l'uno a l'altro stilo."

"O brother, now I see," he said, "the knot that kept the Notary, Guittone, and me short of the sweet new manner that I hear. I clearly see how your pens follow closely behind him who dictates, and certainly that did not happen with our pens; and he who sets himself to ferreting profoundly can find no other difference between the two styles." (Translated by Allen Mandelbaum)

I suffered because of that "now I see," that wistful statement of incapacity, as if to say: look, now I realize there was an obstacle to overcome, and you, Dante, were aware of it and with your writing succeeded in overcoming it, while the Notary, Guittone, and I didn't.

Why does one succeed where others fail? Through lack of inspiration? Through emotional obtuseness, through a lack of intellect and understanding, so to speak, of one's own time? No. It seemed to me, surprisingly, that Bonagiunta made it a matter of speed. I confess that reading those lines made me think of the ordeal of dictation in elementary school, when I was anxious about falling behind — which often happened — and getting lost as the teacher, reading from a text, pronounced the words aloud from her desk. In the same

way the sin of the Notary, Guittone, and Bonagiunta himself appeared to be not that they didn't
listen closely enough to what Love
inspires and dictates but that they
couldn't keep up, as if the transfor-
mation of the voice into writing
were anguishingly slow.

The intensity of that impression on
a reader who longed to write, I
have to say, has not diminished at
all; over the years, given the emphasis on the mystical reading (Mario
Casella, Maria Corti, Davide
Colombo) of Dante's works and
the identification of his sources,
I've been persuaded that what Love
breathes and *dictates within* — so
that later the pen *takes note* and

speaks and shapes — is on the one hand the statement of a poetics but is also, above all, the elucidation of a difficulty. Dante the author, in fact, constructs the episode in such a way that success and failure are two faces of the same coin. The sweet word, in its quantum leap from the interior of the heart to the exterior of writing, needs a swift, capable scribe. If that passage isn't completed with speed — and Bonagiunta admits "your pens follow closely / behind him who dictates, and certainly / that did not happen with our pens" — failure is inevitable. Dante the character knew how to untie himself (Guglielmo Gorni) and as an unfettered scribe was able to write rapidly, keeping up with Love's dictation; while Bonagiunta remained tied and therefore slow, in chains.

What is the nature of the chain that keeps someone from being a rapid scribe? It seemed to me that Dante himself said it implicitly, resorting to the term "style," *stile:* the hand was taught an old style; the Notary, Guittone, and Bonagiunta were trained in that style, as was I, Dante; but now I've been freed from it — it was an inadequate means. The poem dictated by Love requires another style, that is, one with more training, a kind of writing that, with the knots formed earlier untied, seems — as he had written in the *Vita Nuova,* and I had

171

put it down in my notebooks — "almost as if it moved of its own accord" (*quasi come per se stessa mossa*).

I put together passages that were far apart. That *"quasi come"* was, I thought, important. No language and no writing are made by themselves. That is to say: the scribe has to study and become so skillful that it's *almost as if* the word, in becoming writing, were running autonomously from inside to outside, from the heart to the page. The *stil novo,* to be new, had to strive to identify the limits of the old and surpass them, and so achieve writing that would never again miss any of Love's dictation. Bonagiunta —

I said to myself — would have liked to do well but hadn't had the training, the discipline necessary to follow that dictation. Not Dante. He — perhaps more than any other great writer, past or future — knew and feared and fought the inadequacy of writing, in fact considered it part of the limited and transient nature of the human. His very obsession with the new, immediately present in his work, derived from the awareness that writing was chained to writing; that every word had its tradition; that every first language was hatching a second; that from within Cimabue, Giotto emerged; that you had to learn, by yourself or in some school, always starting from the writing of others; that the more disciplined the pen the swifter one became, like an athlete, capable of closely following the voice of Love and seizing what inevitably escaped written tradition; that every form was, in short, a cage, not lasting but necessary if you aspired to write as no one had ever written before.

The Commedia, in this way, seemed to me an extraordinary trap, prepared at great length and in detail. I still think that no writer in the seven hundred years since Dante has succeeded in transforming the living, scholarly analysis of his own time, and the even more scholarly memory of the writings of the past, into a cage so crowded with the life of all humanity and, at the same time, so individually considered, so passionately personal, so specifically local-universal. Someone with a generous mind cited Proust and I tried to convince myself. But I couldn't.

The miraculous snare seemed to me, from those first readings many years ago, identification. On my essential list of a reader longing to write, that was Dante's most astonishing gift. For convenience, I'd like to stay with the encounter with Bonagiunta. I was reading and I was excited: how beautiful is that *i' mi son un,* "I am one who," how effective that proud definition of one's own work. But two lines later — well, I suffered. I suffered for

Bonagiunta and his honest admission of failure. Dante was Dante in the fullness of himself, in his boundless pride as founder of the new; but he was also, at the same time, the Bonagiunta who had been outstripped. He portrayed Bonagiunta's parochialism using the memory of his own parochialism. He presented Bonagiunta's failure reinforcing it with his own distress at not having a lifetime sufficient to learn to do better.

Dante's capacity to situate himself in the other, pivoting on the autobiographical I, with its inherent limits, left me astonished. The secret of his energetic language, which could produce such concise, dazzling phrases, often rapid enough to fix the other in a fleeting gesture, a pose charged with barely perceptible sentiments and resentments, seemed to me principally an effect of identification. A Dantesque description is never merely a description but is always the self transplanted, the heart hurtling swiftly — a few seconds — from inside to out. And certain rapid-fire dialogues, made up of half-line remarks, are a sort of frenetic assignment of contrasting parts. Leaps from within the self to the outside, justified by the comprehension — precisely in the sense of seizing by assimilating — of everything, of the animate and the inanimate, of error and horror.

■ ■ ■ ■

Maybe the power of identification, even too obvious in the poem — like an irrepressible need to shorten distances as much as possible — should be observed not only in Dante the poet-narrator but also in Dante the reader. At school the potency of his similes stunned me. But later, after further study, I learned that those figures often derived from the reading of a great variety of texts. And yet it was never a matter of a pure transcription or a deferential homage or a faithful work of translation. Dante, even when he was reading pagan verses or the Bible or philosophical, scientific, or mystical works, entered into others' words so intimately that he was able to capture their secrets of meaning and beauty, and achieve through them a writing of his own.

Sometimes this operation succeeded and became memorable, sometimes it seemed to fail, as if the original text hadn't dictated enough, or he hadn't noted what was notable with the proper velocity and had missed something. But the verbal energy that Dante released when he positioned himself in a text and then returned to himself with its treasure always seemed to me indisputable, even when the lines, compared with the famous ones, seemed muddled, obscure, if not ugly.

I have to say, in fact, that I found the latter more absorbing. I suspected that confusion and ugliness bore witness to a tendency, on his part, to raise the stakes in every way. In all three canticles I saw the effort of going beyond what he already knew how to imagine and how to do. Sometimes I thought: here not even the most scholarly annotations follow him. I racked my brains and said to myself: he's left behind not only his sense of the beautiful but also ours; we are used to reading and writing too cautiously, we are cowards. Not him, he's seeing if one can make poetry even with the negation of poetry.

To express this extreme impulse

toward identification he left us —
in Paradise 9, where he hypoth-
esizes the celestial happiness of
silent exchanges, a melting and
mixing in the mystic light — words
like *inluiarsi, intuarsi, inmiarsi* (enter
into him, enter into you, enter into
me). They were extremely bold
verbs and so were ill-fated. We
preferred the word that I've used
up to now: *immedesimarsi* (identify
with). And yet in those words I saw
and still see the most intense desire
of the writer and storyteller: the
yearning to untie yourself from
yourself; the dream of becoming
the other without impediment; being yourself while you are me; a
flow of language and writing without feeling otherness as a barrier.

It struck me, however, that Dante hadn't ever invented an *inleiarsi,* enter into her. And yet he was violently attracted to the female, had a pronounced woman's sensibility. (It's relevant, and also rather amusing, that Pound called Dante's rhymes feminine, always accented on the penult.) He had been so bold as to portray himself as being hypersensitive as a Sibyl, his body susceptible from birth to the most nearly invisible signs (Claudio Giunta), to every sort of fragility. And more than anything he had imagined Beatrice, the newest of his novelties.

At this point I'd like to make a small correction. I said that I decided to write this essay out of love for Dante. And it's true. But since I intend to make an effort to speak as "truthfully" as possible — truth is always at the top of a writer's thoughts, especially Dante — I want to explain that that love for Dante immediately became one with his boldest creation: Beatrice. In fact, if I'm faithful to my memories as an adolescent reader, I should add that it was she who made me love Dante right away. I was immediately grateful to him for the way he had portrayed the fearful man, lost in the dark wood, subject to weeping and fainting at the suffering of others, and saved by a believable Florentine woman who started the work of salvation by refusing to greet him and then, having gone to a better life, re-educated him by removing him conclusively from the condition of a delirious child.

Even today I have trouble understanding what he did. Gorni has correctly pointed out that Beatrice "is the only woman in all of Western literature to be invested with such an honorable role." But why does Dante alone place his woman so high in the contemporary hierarchy of the female? What strategies does he use to get to the point of plausibly assigning her such an honor?

For many years I thought that investiture at that level was completely outside the norm of its time.

But in fact Dante was well within the norm. For instance, he ruled out the possibility that she was first of all a woman who engaged in the illustrious act of writing. He considered the gift of eloquence the exclusive property of Adam, from whose first exhalation of breath had come the word: Deus. (Reading *De vulgari eloquentia,* I fantasized that the first woman, lacking her own language, would out of necessity learn the language of the serpent, the only one available, if she wanted to have an understanding of the created world.) He granted no dignity to women's linguistic practices either before or after Babel: they are compared in the *Convivio* to children's. Women, that is, were distinguished for their beauty and their silence, and the young Beatrice of the *Rime* and of a good half of the *Vita Nuova* is no exception.

In daily life Dante portrays her enveloped in her sober-colored garments, reserved and very unlike the decked-out Florentine women denounced by his ancestor Cacciaguida, but so beautiful that she occupied an important place in the hierarchy of desire established by men. In dreams she is silent and naked, that is, covered only by a light crimson cloth, and it's less than convincing that that scarcely concealed nudity is a symbol of purity. She has youthful eyes that dazzle and a mouth that smiles or, if it goes well, offers a restrained salvific greeting that isn't the start of a conversation but inspires muteness and trembling. In other words, the young poet is enfolded within the Provençal feminine, its Siculo-Tuscan adaptation, its Guinizellian reinvention, and the anguished features of Cavalcanti.

But then something starts to change, even before the young woman dies. The moments in the *Vita Nuova* where she stops greeting Dante seemed to me beautiful. And I liked it when, along with her lively friends, Beatrice laughs at him, forcing him, nearly fainting, to lean against a painted wall, as if he himself were nothing but an artifact, a figure among figures, fiction among fictions. But most memorable was the turning point in Chapter 19, when, walking on a path beside a clear stream, Dante is struck by a "great desire to compose a poem" (*tanta volontade di dire*) and a strong impulse to change register, to eliminate the literary convention of enslavement to love and replace it with unrewarded praise of the most gracious lady.

All the textbooks pointed out that passage, and I memorized its importance: it was the start of a long journey of study and consequent self-transformation. But in the end what remained in my mind was that "great desire to compose a poem," which is followed by the eruption (*la mia lingua parlò quasi come per se stessa mossa:* "my tongue spoke almost as if it moved of its own accord") of that first line: *Donne che avete intelletto d'Amore* ("Women who have an understanding of Love"). And so if I'm asked now what does the turning point of Chapter 19 involve, I have trouble answering with formulas like: the historical Beatrice, a person embodied in the "you," now changes into the refined material of Dante's poetic discourse. What immediately occurs to me instead is the strong impression made by that description of the addressees of the *canzone:* "Women who have an understanding of Love": women, that is, who are not "mere females" but have the capacity to understand Love.

I felt that in that famous passage the entire hierarchy of the feminine was rethought, and not in the name of being enslaved to love, and perhaps not even of the gentle heart. The word of Dante's remaking was *intelletto,* "understanding," a word with a complex written tradition, immediately followed, in the position of the objective genitive, by another word — Love — with an equally complex written tradition. Dante was making a truly unexpected leap, evident only if we avoid the interpretation that, in the analysis of the text, opposes the "mere females" to their mutation into symbolic figures. The daughters of Eve remained, overall, a "vulgar crowd." But separated from them were the gracious women — different, that is, from the scornful and sad women, like Micol, of Purgatory 10 — who were endowed with understanding, and probably belonged to the social class sketched in the *Convivio:* human beings, that is, who could not sustain themselves on knowledge not because of an organic flaw or superficiality and laziness but because of "domestic or civic responsibilities." It's an élite that the sensitive, cultured man-poet addresses in the refined poem dictated to him by Love, because he knows that *that* poem will be understood by *those* women. Of course, their language can be only women's, and so by its nature useless. Of course, they can't speak but can only let themselves be praised. And yet they are considered capable of taking in the conceptually complex praise that the poet bestows on them in the person of the one who best sums them up: the not gracious but very gracious Beatrice. Thus, once sexual attraction and the hierarchy of beauty were set aside, the young author of the *Vita Nuova* could inaugurate a new hierarchy of women based on the capacity to understand. Eliminating the sexual purposes but preserving the category of gracious women whose beauty still agitated the equally gracious hearts of men, Dante singled out a category of women to whom one could express, offer as reading, or sing demanding thoughts, knowing they would be understood.

If he had stopped there, he would, in my view, already have performed within the limits of his time a remarkable feat as a man promoting women's potential. But, as we know, he didn't stop. Or at least so I thought during high school and university.

Maybe he realized that the world of women wasn't only the one right before his eyes: mothers crushed by domestic responsibilities, girls watched over by husbands, poor young women exposed to every sort of violence, women with dissolute behavior, or even gracious women like Francesca, carried away by reading chivalric romances. Maybe, already in the last lines of the *Vita Nuova,* he had realized that certain women could have more complex characters, that there were radically and daringly new female figures, much newer than those — also very new — he considered to be capable of understanding Love. And so he ended his book resolving not to write about Beatrice anymore, until he had found a way to further distort the old forms and "say of her what had never been said about any woman."

He will do it. It'll take a few years, some manly wandering, and a great deal of study. But when Beatrice reappears in the Commedia she will no longer be merely a woman who is able to understand Love, nor will she be only the most gracious. In a stroke of genius, Dante changes her radically by having her emerge from her muteness, as Bianca Garavelli notes in her commentary on the poem. I don't know if this has received more than a mention elsewhere, but certainly it deserves to; to me, at least, it seemed a fundamental fact that Dante based the monument to the girl from Florence on the gift of speech.

Beatrice spoke now, and she didn't speak in the paltry modes of the language of women or offer a brief greeting. Beatrice spoke like a man and perhaps better. For example, as if she were Dante himself, she declares, in the account offered by Virgil in Inferno 2: "Love moved me, which makes me speak." And in Purgatory 30 she makes a radical verbal leap that amazed me. Dante, in short, had done his utmost. In order to say of her what had never been said of any woman, he had *extinguished* the first, flawless language of Adam, had joined those who said it is "nature's act" that man and woman speak (Paradise 26), and had given to Bice Portinari, who, being dead, was now indisputably unconnected to the "mere females," not only a seat in heaven but an extraordinary eloquence and knowledge.

■ ■ ■ ■

Here we are, then, at the point that excited me most and still does: Beatrice, between Limbo and Eden and celestial spheres, becomes an unquestioned authority, deliberately mixing the feminine and the masculine. In her tones she is lover, mother, and, surprisingly, admiral. In her otherworldly life, she has a status that allows her to ascribe to the male first-person narrator, the protagonist of the "vision," an exemplary quality not different from that of St. Augustine or Boethius. Her authority as the lady of heaven is such that she can legitimately bestow on that first-person narrator, after a journey lasting some sixty-four cantos, the same name as the author: Dante.

And it's only the start. Right afterward, precisely by virtue of her hierarchical placement, Beatrice can dare to reproach her man with the harshness of a woman who has gone on, literally, to a better life, that is, a life that is no longer confined in the body of the beautiful girl with youthful eyes but lives in that of the now fully complete person. Her reprimand has all the features of retaliation. It's as if she were saying: look at me, here's what I potentially was and you didn't understand the change in me, you were stuck at a stage that no longer concerned me. The sin, that is, for which Dante now has to shed tears of repentance, is that he remained with the image that he himself developed of the forever childlike gracious woman; that he didn't learn from the dissolution of that image; that he in fact lingered to dig it up again, with *pargolette,* young girls, who by their nature cannot have a strong awareness of self or of Love, but are at most capable of a silent comprehension of the male language of praise. See here instead with what awareness and knowledge and speech a woman who is no longer constrained by the knots of earthly life knows how to *abbellarsi,* adorn herself.

Where did Dante get the elements

to invent this definitive Beatrice? Scholarship in the last thirty years of the twentieth century — I learned — demonstrated generally how female roles, in the Middle Ages, were more varied and complex than males would admit in their courtship. There were cultured women, there were women who at risk and danger to themselves read and commented on the Scriptures. And in fact, if we patiently go through the list of how many complex matters the poet-philosopher — he who in the *Convivio* had distributed, democratically, knowledge to men and especially women with little time for contemplation and many responsibilities, composing *canzoni* dense with knowledge and meaning and learnedly commenting on them — ascribes to Beatrice's authority, we are amazed. I still am. And I'd like to compare Dante to Meister Eckhart as Luisa Muraro, in her *Il Dio delle donne* [*The God of Women*], sketched him, on the wave of a series of end-of-the-century studies on the feminine mystique. As Eckhart in his writings absorbs the experience of the Beguines, so Dante could have reinvented Beatrice poetically by looking at the scholarly women who were commenting on the Scriptures. It's not a matter of confirming the cliché of Beatrice as the symbol of Theology. Beatrice is not (only) a symbol. Dante imagines her, literally, as a woman who has an understanding of God and speculative language, modeling her — I like to think — in the likeness of such figures as Mechthild of Magdeburg, Hildegard of Bingen, Juliana of Norwich, Marguerite Porete, and Angela da Foligno, *magistra theologorum.* He does it naturally by bestowing on a female figure scientific, theological, mystical knowledge that is his, that he gets from his studies, from his rib. But in doing this — in that *inleiarsi,* so to speak, entering into, becoming her — he ventures to imagine, with his mystic-leaning rationalism, with his visionary realism, what is possible for women. And for this we should be grateful to him. With that monument he did more than many others over the centuries. So what if "Dante" — the first word of that speech of Beatrice's invented in Purgatory 30 — sounds a little like a calque of the word God in Adam's mouth, when the figure of dust that is the first man receives from his creator the gift of speech and, for the first time, devoutly, speaks to him.

ABOUT THE AUTHORS

Elena Ferrante is the author of *The Days of Abandonment* (Europa, 2005), *Troubling Love* (Europa, 2006), and *The Lost Daughter* (Europa, 2008), now a film directed by Maggie Gyllenhaal and starring Olivia Colman, Dakota Johnson, and Paul Mescal. She is also the author of *Incidental Inventions* (Europa, 2019), illustrated by Andrea Ucini, *Frantumaglia: A Writer's Journey* (Europa, 2016), and a children's picture book illustrated by Mara Cerri, *The Beach at Night* (Europa, 2016). The four volumes known as the "Neapolitan quartet" (*My Brilliant Friend, The Story of a New Name, Those Who Leave and Those Who Stay,* and *The Story of the Lost Child*) were published by Europa Editions in English between 2012 and 2015. *My Brilliant Friend,* the HBO series directed by Saverio Costanzo, premiered in 2018. Ferrante's most recent novel, the *New York Times* bestselling *The Lying Life of Adults,* was published in 2020 by Europa Editions.

Ann Goldstein has translated all of Elena Ferrante's books, including the *New York Times* bestseller

The Lying of Adults and the international bestseller *My Brilliant Friend.* She has been honored with a Guggenheim Fellowship and is the recipient of the PEN Renato Poggioli Translation Award. She lives in New York.